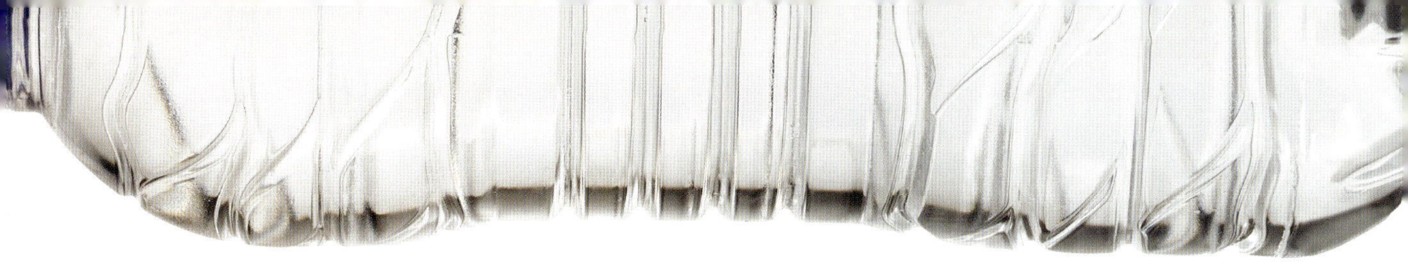

Clever Crafts with PLASTIC BOTTLES

by Chelsey Luciow

raintree
a Capstone company — publishers for children

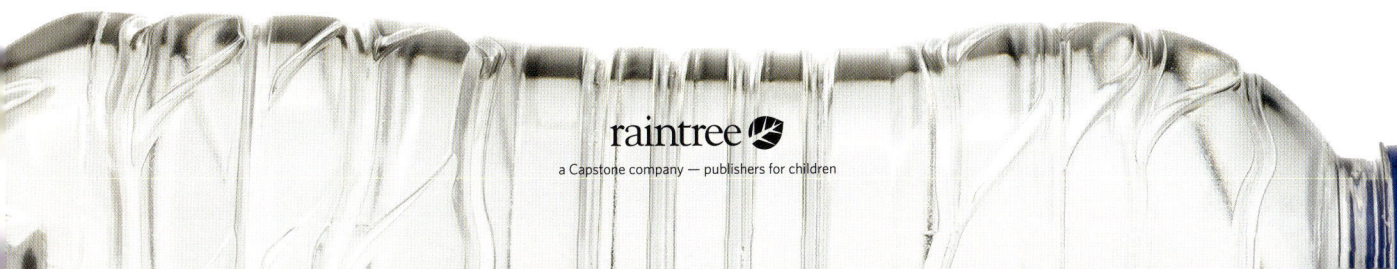

Raintree is an imprint of Capstone Global Library Limited, a company incorporated in England and Wales having its registered office at 264 Banbury Road, Oxford, OX2 7DY – Registered company number: 6695582

www.raintree.co.uk
myorders@raintree.co.uk

Text © Capstone Global Library Limited 2025
The moral rights of the proprietor have been asserted.

All rights reserved. No part of this publication may be reproduced in any form or by any means (including photocopying or storing it in any medium by electronic means and whether or not transiently or incidentally to some other use of this publication) without the written permission of the copyright owner, except in accordance with the provisions of the Copyright, Designs and Patents Act 1988 or under the terms of a licence issued by the Copyright Licensing Agency, 5th Floor, Shackleton House, 4 Battle Bridge Lane, London SE1 2HX (www.cla.co.uk). Applications for the copyright owner's written permission should be addressed to the publisher.

Edited by Jessica Rusick
Designed by Denise Hamernik
Original illustrations © Capstone Global Library Limited 2025
Originated by Capstone Global Library Ltd

978 1 3982 5993 5

British Library Cataloguing in Publication Data
A full catalogue record for this book is available from the British Library.

Acknowledgements
We would like to thank the following for permission to reproduce photographs: Adobe Stock: DenisProduction.com, 23 (tealights), Mighty Media, Inc.: project photos; Shutterstock: Scisetti Alfio, 4. Design elements: Adobe Stock: mspoint; Shutterstock: AlenKadr

Every effort has been made to contact copyright holders of material reproduced in this book. Any omissions will be rectified in subsequent printings if notice is given to the publisher.

All the internet addresses (URLs) given in this book were valid at the time of going to press. However, due to the dynamic nature of the internet, some addresses may have changed, or sites may have changed or ceased to exist since publication. While the author and publisher regret any inconvenience this may cause readers, no responsibility for any such changes can be accepted by either the author or the publisher.

All product and company names are trademarks™ or registered® trademarks of their respective holders.

The publisher and the author shall not be liable for any damages allegedly arising from the information in this book, and they specifically disclaim any liability from the use or application of any of the contents of this book.

Printed and bound in India.

Contents

Clever plastic bottle crafts! 4
Waterless flowers. 6
Feed the frog game 8
Jellyfish mobile 10
Elegant earrings 12
Trainer safety pin. 14
Animal cap cards 16
Art supply organizer 18
Super spinner 20
Luminous lanterns 22
Custom cityscape 24
Robot canister 26
Bottle flip planters 28
Cap magnets 30
    Find out more 32
    About the author 32

Clever PLASTIC BOTTLE CRAFTS!

Plastic bottles are not just for holding liquids. They are the perfect crafting material! With a little creativity, you can turn plain old plastic bottles into a stylish mobile, pretty earrings or petite planters. Gather plastic bottles from your space. Then use them to make clever crafts!

All about plastic bottles

Plastic bottles come in many shapes, sizes and colours. One common type of plastic used to make bottles is polyethylene terephthalate (PET). PET is lightweight and strong. Water bottles, fizzy drinks bottles, cooking oil bottles and more are made from PET.

Basic supplies

- beads
- card stock
- hairdryer
- hot-glue gun and glue sticks
- paint and paintbrushes
- pencil
- plastic bottles
- PVA glue (white and clear)
- ruler
- scissors
- tissue paper

Crafting tips

1. **Get ready.** Gather all the supplies and read through the instructions carefully before starting a project. Cover your workspace with newspaper or plastic to protect it from messes.

2. **Ask first.** Get permission to use any supplies you find.

3. **Stay safe.** Ask an adult for help using hot or sharp tools.

4. **Be creative.** Project steps are only a guide. Use different materials or try new things to make the project your own!

5. **Tidy up.** Clean your space once you have finished crafting. Put supplies back where you found them and wipe down your crafting surface.

WATERLESS FLOWERS

SUPPLIES
- plastic bottles
- scissors
- heavy, flat item such as a book
- paint and paintbrushes
- paint pens
- hot-glue gun and glue sticks
- wooden dowels
- large beads (optional)
- plastic jar
- duct tape
- pebbles or beans

These pretty plastic flowers will brighten up any space!

1. Cut the bottles in half width-wise. Make several slices down each bottle-half to create petals. Put something heavy on the petals to help them stay open.

2. Paint the bottles in solid colours. You can paint the inside, outside or both depending on what looks best to you. Let the paint dry.

3. Use paint pens to add designs such as polka dots and stripes to the flowers.

4. If you like, you could hot-glue different flower pieces together to create depth in your flower designs.

5. Use wooden dowels for stems. Cut a hole in each flower and push the dowel through. You can also hot-glue a large bead into a bottle neck opening and then glue the stem to the bead. Paint the stems different colours.

6. Decorate the jar with paint pens and duct tape for a vase. Then fill the vase with pebbles or beans. Arrange your flowers in the vase!

FEED THE FROG GAME

Craft this simple game for hours of frog-tastic fun!

SUPPLIES

- 1.5-litre plastic bottle with cap
- scissors
- green paint and paintbrush
- extra bottle cap
- hot-glue gun and glue sticks
- beads
- craft foam (green and black)
- green marker pen
- googly eyes
- red wool
- ruler

1. Cut off the bottom half of the bottle and set it aside. Cut two triangle shapes on either side of the top half to create an open mouth.

2. Paint the inside of the bottle green. Let the paint dry.

3. Create the fly with the extra bottle cap. Cut two small wings from the bottom half of the bottle. Hot glue them to the cap. Hot-glue on two beads for eyes.

4. Sketch frog legs and arched eye shapes on the green craft foam. The eye shapes should be large enough to fit googly eyes. Cut out all the shapes.

5. Cut a slit at the bottom of the foam eye shapes. This will help you attach them to the bottle. Glue eyes onto the shapes.

6. Hot-glue the foam pieces onto the frog. The eyes should go above the mouth and the legs should go on either side.

7. Tie a knot at one end of a 50-cm piece of wool. Hot-glue the knot to the bottom of the bottle's cap. String the wool through the frog and twist the cap on the bottle. Tie a knot at the other end of the wool. Hot-glue the knot to the bottom of the fly. Cut a small circle of black craft foam and hot-glue it on top of the knot to reinforce it.

8. Now you're ready to play! See how many times you can swing the fly into the frog's mouth.

JELLYFISH MOBILE

SUPPLIES

- 3 plastic bottles (500 ml) with caps
- scissors
- permanent marker pens
- clip
- ruler
- hairdryer
- hot-glue gun and glue sticks
- small beads
- bottom of 2-litre bottle
- paint and paintbrush
- wool or string
- duct tape

Pretend you're under the sea with this eye-catching mobile.

1. Cut the top and bottom off the small bottles. Cut the middle section into two pieces.

2. Colour the middle pieces with permanent marker pens. Colour the three bottom bottle sections as well. Each one will be the body of a jellyfish.

3. Flatten out the middle pieces. Cut fringe along one long end of each piece. The cuts should be about 0.5 cm apart. Clip the non-fringed end of each piece so it stays flat. Use a hairdryer to warm up the fringe. It should curl slightly. These are the jellyfish's tentacles.

4. Roll up the non-fringed end of each piece. Hot-glue the roll to the inside of each bottle cap so the tentacles stick out. Hot-glue each cap into the inside of a body. Hot-glue a small bead to the top of each body.

5. Paint the inside of the 2-litre bottle bottom and let it dry. This will be the mobile's top. String wool or string through the beads at the top of each jellyfish and tie a double knot. Tape the knots to the inside of the mobile top.

6. Tape three loops of wool or string to the top of the mobile. Knot the wool or string ends together and hang your mobile.

ELEGANT EARRINGS

SUPPLIES

- clear plastic bottle
- scissors
- permanent marker pens
- paintbrush or wooden dowel
- hairdryer
- clothes pegs
- awl or pin
- needle-nose pliers
- metal rings
- earring hooks

These chic spiral earrings are bound to make an impression.

1. Cut a section of the plastic bottle that is smooth to work on. Use the permanent marker pens to draw a design on one side.

2. Cut a slice of the design and wrap it around a paintbrush handle or wooden dowel. Use clothes pegs to hold the plastic in place.

3. Heat the plastic with the hairdryer for one to two minutes. Let the plastic cool for two minutes before removing the clothes pegs.

4. Repeat steps 2 and 3 to create the other earring.

5. Carefully poke a hole at the top of each earring with the awl or pin.

6. Open the metal rings with the pliers and hook each one through an earring hole. Hook an earring hook onto each ring. Close the rings using the pliers and try your new earrings on!

CLEVER TIP

Create more earrings! Try cutting slices of different thicknesses or wrapping the plastic in new shapes.

TRAINER SAFETY PIN

SUPPLIES

- plastic bottles (clear or coloured)
- scissors
- permanent marker pens
- hole punch (optional)
- awl or pin
- safety pins
- needle-nose pliers
- beads

Add bling to your wardrobe with these stylish safety pins.

1. Cut the plastic bottle into smooth strips that are about 10 cm × 2.5 cm. Decorate the strips with marker pen designs on one side.

2. Cut the plastic into different shapes using scissors or a hole punch.

3. Use an awl or pin to poke holes in the plastic shapes.

4. Open the safety pin. Use the pliers to loosen the coiled part of the pin. Open it up enough so that beads can be pushed over the coil.

5. Thread beads and plastic pieces onto the safety pin.

6. Once the pin is full, use the pliers to realign and tighten the coil so the beads and plastic pieces won't fall off. Wear your pins on your shoelaces, or even on a backpack or jacket!

ANIMAL CAP CARDS

SUPPLIES
- plastic bottle caps
- paint and paintbrushes
- paint pens
- scissors
- coloured paper
- hot-glue gun and glue sticks
- decorations
- glue stick
- pen
- permanent marker pens
- blank cards or folded card stock

Wish a friend or family member well with these cute and clever bottle-cap cards.

1. Use paint or paint pens to colour the cap the colour of your chosen animal.

2. Cut out a 7.5-cm square of coloured paper. Hot-glue the bottle cap to the centre of the square of paper. Add decorations such as foam stickers, googly eyes, smaller bottle caps or wings cut from scrap plastic to complete the animal.

3. Cut a 10-cm square of coloured paper. Glue the paper from step 2 to it. Then glue the layered papers to the front of the card.

4. Use pen and permanent marker pens to write a friendly, animal-themed message on another piece of coloured paper. Glue it to the front of the card!

CLEVER TIP

Use permanent marker pen to add 2D elements such as legs or antennae to your bottle-cap animals.

ART SUPPLY ORGANIZER

SUPPLIES

- plastic bottles with flat backs (washing-up liquid bottles work well)
- elastic bands
- permanent marker pens
- scissors
- duct tape
- greaseproof paper
- patterned tape

Use plastic bottles to brighten and organize your space!

1. Put an elastic band around each bottle about two-thirds of the way up as a guideline for cutting. Trace the elastic bands on the front sides only. Draw a line up and around the back of each bottle, above the rubber band, for the handle. Draw an oval below the handle lines for the handles' openings.

2. Cut the lines you made in step 1. Cover the bottles in duct tape. Cut slits into the tape to help it wrap around curves more easily.

3. Wrap greaseproof paper over each bottle. Trace the front of each bottle on the greaseproof paper so you know how much room you have for your design.

4. Write or draw a design on the greaseproof paper. You might choose to label the supplies or write art-inspired words.

5. Use patterned tape to cover your design. Turn the greaseproof paper over and use the back to guide your cutting. Cut out the design.

6. Peel the letters off the greaseproof paper and attach them to the bottles. Display the bottles on a desk or hang them by their handles!

SUPER SPINNER

SUPPLIES

- plastic water bottles with caps
- permanent marker pens
- scissors
- scrap wood
- hammer and nail
- string

Hang this plastic spiral spinner in a sunny outside spot!

20

1. Use permanent marker pens to draw a design on the bottle.

2. Cut off the bottom of the bottle and set it aside. Cut the rest of the bottle into a spiral. Start from the bottom and cut at a slight angle around the entire bottle until you reach the neck.

3. Repeat steps 1 and 2 to create several spiralled bottles.

4. Put the bottle caps on some scrap wood. Use the hammer and nail to hammer a hole in the centre of each bottle cap. Ask a trusted adult to help you with this step – do not try this on your own.

5. Thread one piece of string through all but one cap and tie a knot at the top of the last cap threaded. Then thread the bottom of the string through the bottle necks.

6. Thread the bottom of the string through the last bottle cap and tie a knot.

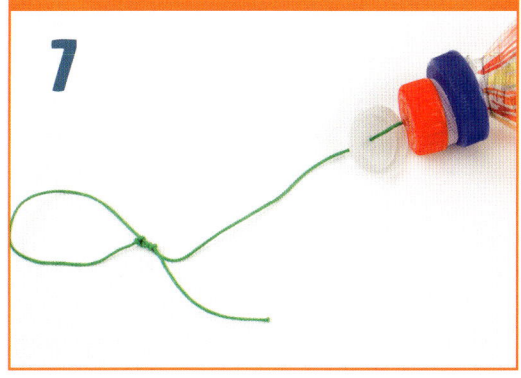

7. Tie a loop at the top of the string. Then hang your plastic bottle spinner!

CLEVER TIP

String bells on the spinner to turn it into a wind chime!

LUMINOUS LANTERNS

Brighten any space with these colourful light-up lanterns.

SUPPLIES

- tissue paper
- scissors
- large plastic bottles
- white PVA glue
- water
- paper cup
- paintbrush
- wire
- ruler
- needle-nose pliers
- hole punch
- battery-powered tealights

1. Fold tissue paper of different colours and cut out different shapes.

2. Cut the top halves off the bottles.

3. Mix two parts glue to one part water in the cup. Use a paintbrush to apply the mixture to the outside of the bottle. Stick the tissue paper shapes to the glue. Then brush on another glue layer to seal in the shapes.

4. Cut a length of wire about 50 cm long for each handle. Use pliers to make curls and twists in the wire.

5. Punch holes into two opposite sides of each bottle for the handle. Loop the ends of the wire through the holes and twist to secure.

6. Add electric tealights to the lanterns and display them. (Do not use wax tealights with a real flame.)

CUSTOM CITYSCAPE

SUPPLIES

- several plastic bottles of different sizes
- scissors
- masking tape
- paint and paintbrushes
- cotton bud (optional)
- hot-glue gun and glue sticks
- paint pens

Craft your own plastic bottle city for play or display.

1. Experiment with different shapes for your cityscape. Cut the bottles to different heights and turn them upside down for buildings. Use bottle tops, bottoms or other pieces to create roofs and other features.

2. Place masking tape pieces on the fronts of the buildings for windows. Consider making the windows different shapes and sizes.

3. Paint the buildings and roofs. Once they are dry, peel off the tape. Use the cotton bud to clean paint from the windows if needed.

4. Hot-glue the roofs to the tops of buildings.

5. Use paint pens to add details to the buildings and roofs. Draw windowpanes, doors and roof tiles. Think about using different colours to create variety!

ROBOT CANISTER

SUPPLIES

- 2 plastic bottles of the same size
- scissors
- paint and paintbrushes
- 2 bottle caps
- scrap wood
- hammer and nail
- push pin
- split pins
- plastic confetti mix
- zip
- duct tape

Turn plastic bottles into a cute storage canister!

1. Cut the top halves off each bottle. The two bottoms will be used for the robot.

2. Paint the outside of each bottle. After the first layer is dry, paint on details such as eyes and buttons. One bottle will be the head and the other will be the body.

3. Put the bottle caps on scrap wood. Use the hammer and nail to punch a hole in the inside rim of each cap. Ask a trusted adult to help you with this step – do not try this on your own. These will be the robot's ears. Use a push pin to poke holes in the robot's head for the ears. Use split pins to connect the ears to the head. Open the split pins inside the head.

4. Use split pins and confetti to create eyes. Poke a hole through a piece of confetti and then through the bottle for each eye. Push split pins through the holes. Open the split pins inside the bottle.

5. Tape one side of the zip to the inside rim of the body. Make sure the zip is facing out. Unzip the zip. Tape the other side of the zip to the inside rim of the head. Put anything you like into the canister. Then close the zip to store your items!

BOTTLE FLIP PLANTERS

SUPPLIES
- plastic bottles with caps
- scissors
- spray paint
- scrap wood
- hammer and nail
- wire
- beads
- pipe cleaners
- pebbles
- planting soil
- small plants

These pleasant plastic planters will add a pop of freshness to any space.

1. Cut the bottom off a plastic bottle. The top should be about 15 cm long with the cap on.

2. Spray paint the bottle. Let it dry.

3. Put the cap on scrap wood. Hammer a hole into the centre of the cap. Ask a trusted adult to help you with this step – do not try this on your own. Put the cap back on the bottle. Thread a wire approximately 50 cm long through the cap and into the bottle. Add beads to the cap end of the wire and twist the wire to secure the beads. The other end of the wire will be used to hang the planter later.

4. Twist the ends of two pipe cleaners together. Wrap them around the bottle's neck. Loop the pipe cleaners up the planter and hook the ends to the lip of the planter.

5. Add pebbles to the planter for drainage. Add potting soil on top.

6. Carefully add a plant to the soil.

7. Repeat steps 1–6 to create more planters. Twist the hanging wires around a nail or hook to hang them!

CAP MAGNETS

SUPPLIES
- plastic bottle caps
- pencil
- card stock
- patterned paper
- scissors
- glue stick
- waterproof pen
- stickers (optional)
- clear PVA glue
- decorations, such as plastic confetti pieces
- toothpick
- hot-glue gun and glue sticks
- magnets
- plastic bottle (optional)

Stick these bottle cap magnets on a fridge, locker or anywhere else that could use a little flair.

1. Trace the bottle cap on both card stock and patterned paper. Cut out the circles and glue them together as the background of your magnet design.

2. Write a message on the patterned paper circle with a waterproof pen. Add stickers if you like.

3. Pour a small amount of clear PVA glue into the cap and place the paper circle inside. Pour more glue on top. The paper should be covered but glue should not spill out of the cap. Tilt the cap in different directions to make sure the entire design is covered in glue.

4. Add decorations to the cap while the glue is still wet. Use a toothpick to carefully adjust the decorations so the message can still be read clearly.

5. Allow the glue to dry for at least three hours. Once it is dry, hot-glue a magnet to the back of the cap. If you like, cut shapes from a plastic bottle and hot-glue them around the magnet for extra dimension. Repeat steps 1–5 to make more magnets!

Find out more

Books

10-Minute Crafty Projects (10-Minute Makers), Elsie Olson (Raintree, 2021)

Eco Craft Book: Don't Throw It Away, Recreate & Play, Laura Minter and Tia Williams (GMC Publications, 2021)

Upcycled Plastic Projects (Eco Crafts), Marcy Morin and Heidi E. Thompson (Raintree, 2022)

Websites

www.bbc.co.uk/cbbc/curations/bp-arts-and-crafts-collection
Love crafting? Head for the CBBC Blue Peter arts and crafts collection.

www.goodhousekeeping.com/home/craft-ideas/g20967550/summer-crafts/
Check out this website for lots of different craft ideas for you to try.

About the author

Chelsey Luciow is an artist and creator. She loves reading with children and believes books are magical. Chelsey lives with her wife, their son and their dogs.